The Sun

by Martha E. H. Rustad

CAPSTONE PRESS
a capstone imprint

Little Pebble is published by Capstone Press,
1710 Roe Crest Drive, North Mankato, Minnesota 56003
www.capstonepub.com

Library of Congress Cataloging-in-Publication Data
Rustad, Martha E. H. (Martha Elizabeth Hillman), 1975– author.
  The sun / by Martha E. H. Rustad.
      pages cm.—(Little pebble. Space)
  Audience: Ages 5–7.
  Audience: K to grade 3.
  Summary: "Simple text and full-color photographs describe the Sun"—Provided by
the publisher.
  Includes bibliographical references and index.
  ISBN 978-1-4914-8324-4 (library binding)
  ISBN 978-1-4914-8328-2 (paperback)
  ISBN 978-1-4914-8332-9 (eBook PDF)
  1. Sun—Juvenile literature. I. Title.
  QB521.5.R87 2016
  523.7—dc23   2015023302

Editorial Credits
Erika L. Shores, editor; Juliette Peters and Katelin Plekkenpol, designers;
Tracy Cummins, media researcher; Katy LaVigne, production specialist

Photo Credits
Getty Images: Juice Images, 5; Science Source: Eric Cohen, 13, Mark Garlick, 9; Shutterstock:
Kalenik Hanna, Design Element, lassedesignen, 19, Mopic, 15, Paul Fleet, 17, PaulPaladin, 11,
Triff, Cover, 1, 7, Zurijeta, 21

Editor's Note
In this book's photographs, the sizes of objects and the distances between them
are not to scale.

Printed in the United States of America.
120318 001317

Table of Contents

About the Sun

The sun shines.

Feel its heat.

See its light.

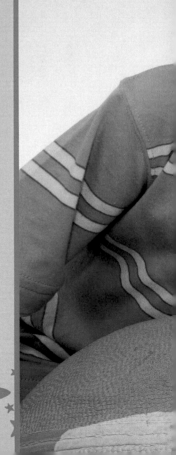

What is the sun?

A star!

Stars are balls

of burning gases.

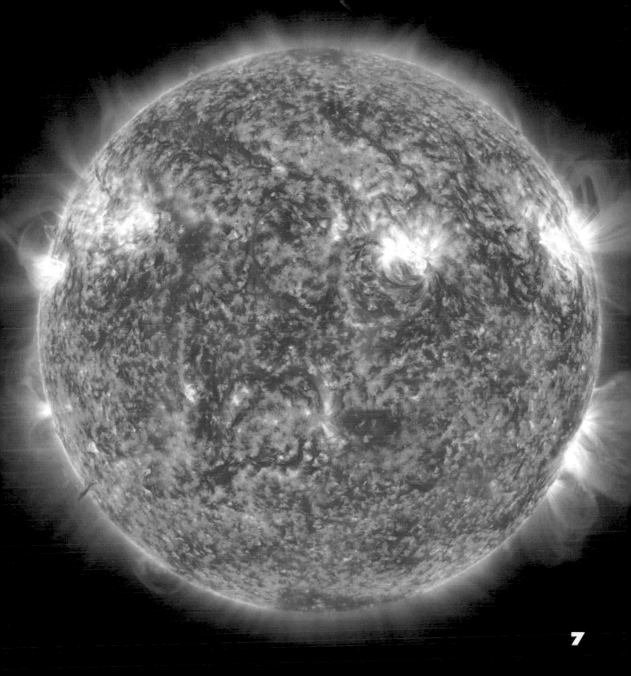

The Sun's Place

The sun sits in
the Milky Way.
Our galaxy looks
like a disk.

How far away is the sun?
About 93 million miles
(150 million kilometers)!

Big and Hot

The sun is huge.

It is as wide as 109 Earths.

Earth

sun

13

Inside the sun is the core.

The sun is hottest there.

core

Solar flares shoot out.

Hot gases escape.

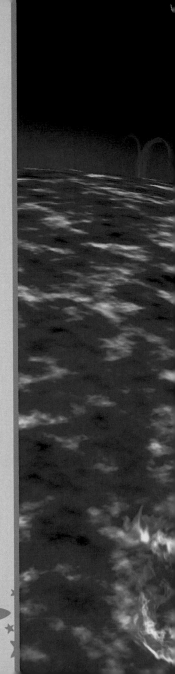

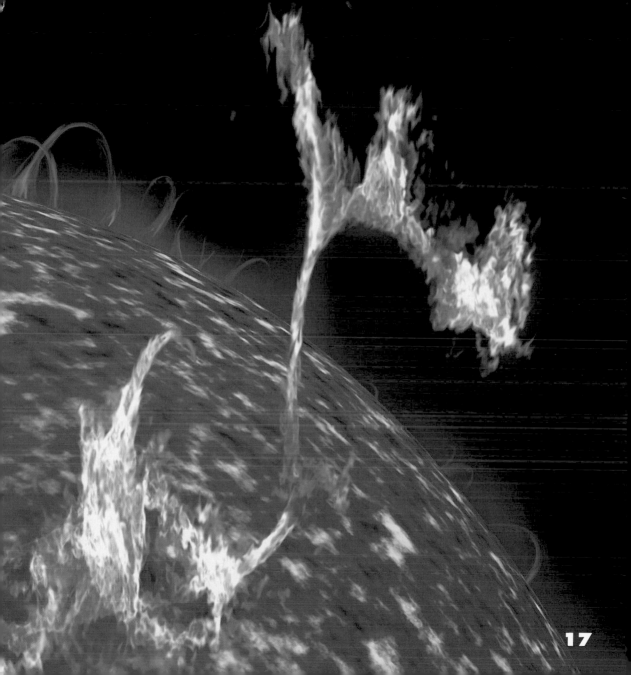

The Sun and Earth

The sun always shines.

Earth turns. Our side faces

the sun. It is day.

Our side turns away.

It is night.

We need the sun.

Its heat warms Earth.

Its rays light Earth.

Thank you, sun!

Glossary

galaxy—a large group of billions of stars

gas—a substance that spreads to fill any space that holds it

planet—a large object in space that orbits a star

ray—a line of light and heat

solar flare—a burst of energy and gas from the sun's surface

star—a ball of burning gases; the sun is a star

Read More

Bredeson, Carmen, and Marianne Dyson. *Exploring the Sun.* Launch into Space! New York: Enslow Publishing LLC, 2015.

Flynn, Claire. *A Trip to the Sun.* Fantastic Science Journeys. New York: Gareth Stevens Publishing, 2015.

Glaser, Chaya. *The Sun: A Super Star.* Out of this World. New York: Bearport Publishing, 2015.

Internet Sites

FactHound offers a safe, fun way to find Internet sites related to this book. All of the sites on FactHound have been researched by our staff.

Here's all you do:
Visit *www.facthound.com*
Type in this code: 9781491483244

 Check out projects, games and lots more at
www.capstonekids.com

Index